EARLY LEA[...]

STICKER STORY BOOKS

Going Shopping

GILLIAN HALLSWORTH

ILLUSTRATED · BY · DEREK · MATTHEWS

A Piccolo Original
Piccolo Books

This series has been prepared in consultation with the Pre-school Playgroups Association.

Jenny
Anthony
Megan
Kirsty
SUNFLOWER WAY
2
1
3
Thomas
Paula
Andrew

Michael
Graham
Alistair
Ling
Sunflower Stores
5
6
4
7
Aunty Lola
Han
8

At number two Sunflower Way, Paula and her Mummy are getting ready to go to the shops.
Paula has drawn some of the things they need to buy.

What do you take with you when you go shopping?

Can you walk to the shops?

Point to the things you need to take on a shopping trip.

First stop is the toy shop.
They have to buy a birthday present for Ling.
Paula just can't decide . . . Then they see a beautiful xylophone.
That will do nicely.

Choose something from the toy shop.

Which xylophone is different from the others? Why?

Do you have any musical instruments? What are they called?

Next door at the greengrocer's,
they buy a cauliflower and some carrots.
Paula looks carefully at her list.
Oh yes, some apples, please.
What can you see in this shop?

What are your favourite vegetables and fruit?

How many apples can you see?

How many bananas? How many carrots?

Are there more apples or more carrots?

Those chickens look good today.
Mummy asks the butcher for a large one.
Paula reminds her to buy some sausages.
What do you usually eat for your lunch?

Try to find someone else from Sunflower Way in this picture.

How many sausages are there?

Which is the longest sausage? Which is the fattest?

Which is the biggest chicken?

Which is the smallest?

How many chickens?

Mmm . . . what a delicious smell coming from the baker's shop. Mummy asks for a brown loaf and two rather special cakes — one for Paula and one for Anthony.

What sort of bread can you see? Who is Anthony?

Point to the baker
the butcher
the greengrocer.

Who is the tallest?
Who has curly hair?

On to the post office to buy some stamps.
Paula is still too little to see over the counter.
She can stick a stamp on the letter though.

What colour are letter boxes?

Try to find someone else from Sunflower Way in this picture.

Put the stamps back together.

At the supermarket Mummy hangs her basket on the trolley.
Paula finds her list.
Let's see . . . the eggs are over there.
Do you know why eggs are packed in cartons?

Which is the tin?

Which is the jar?

Can you talk about the other containers? What are they called?

What do you think is in each of the containers?

Up and down the aisles they go.
Mummy finds the spaghetti.
Paula finds her favourite yoghurts.
Put them in the trolley very carefully, Paula!

What can you see in Paula's trolley?
What do you usually eat for your tea?

Try to find someone else from Sunflower Way in this picture.

There are five more yoghurts hidden in this picture. Can you find them?

They've finished at last.
Paula helps to unload the shopping at the checkout.
Oh dear. There isn't enough money in Paula's purse.
Mummy will have to pay!

Why does Mummy put the eggs and yoghurt on top of her basket?

Help Paula and her Mummy to find their way out of the supermarket.

At home, they put everything away in the right places.
Then they sit down for a rest.
Mummy drinks her coffee and Paula
has some apple juice.

Where do you keep yoghurt . . . eggs . . . apples . . . soap powder?

Find which straw belongs to which container.

There are five differences in these two pictures.

Try to spot them all.